D0690093

Makers as INNOVATORS JUNIOR

Coding with Lego WeDo

By Amy Quinn

Published in the United States of America by
Cherry Lake Publishing
Ann Arbor, Michigan
www.cherrylakepublishing.com

Series Editor: Kristin Fontichiaro
Photo Credits: All photos by Amy Quinn

Library of Congress Cataloging-in-Publication Data has been filed and is available at catalog.loc.gov

Cherry Lake Publishing would like to acknowledge the work of the Partnership for 21st Century Learning. Please visit *www.p21.org* for more information.

Printed in the United States of America
Corporate Graphics

A Note to Adults: Please review the instructions for the activities in this book before allowing children to do them. Be sure to help them with any activities you do not think they can safely complete on their own.

A Note to Kids: Be sure to ask an adult for help with these activities when you need it. Always put your safety first!

Table of Contents

Make your Lego pieces move! A computer or tablet, Lego bricks, and simple motors bring your creations to life.

Introduction

Imagine building a Lego model that can move or make sounds! You can do this in just a few simple steps using the Lego Education WeDo 2.0 Core Set. Read this book to find out how to program and build **motorized** Lego models. You will be amazed when your model moves!

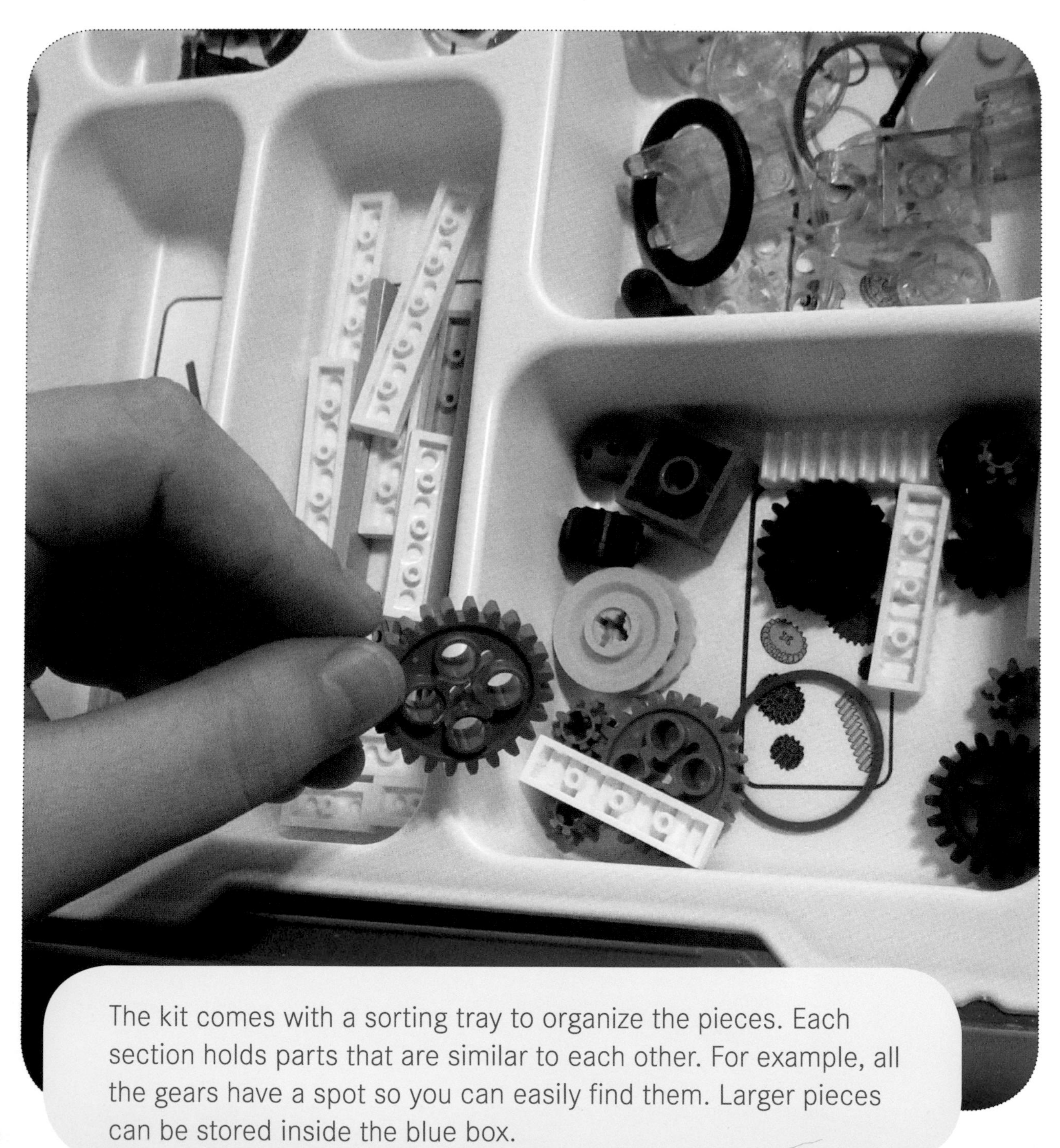

The kit comes with a sorting tray to organize the pieces. Each section holds parts that are similar to each other. For example, all the gears have a spot so you can easily find them. Larger pieces can be stored inside the blue box.

Materials

You will need the following items to complete Lego WeDo projects:

- Lego WeDo 2.0 Core Set
- Tablet or other computer
- Lego WeDo 2.0 **software**
- Extra Lego pieces (optional)

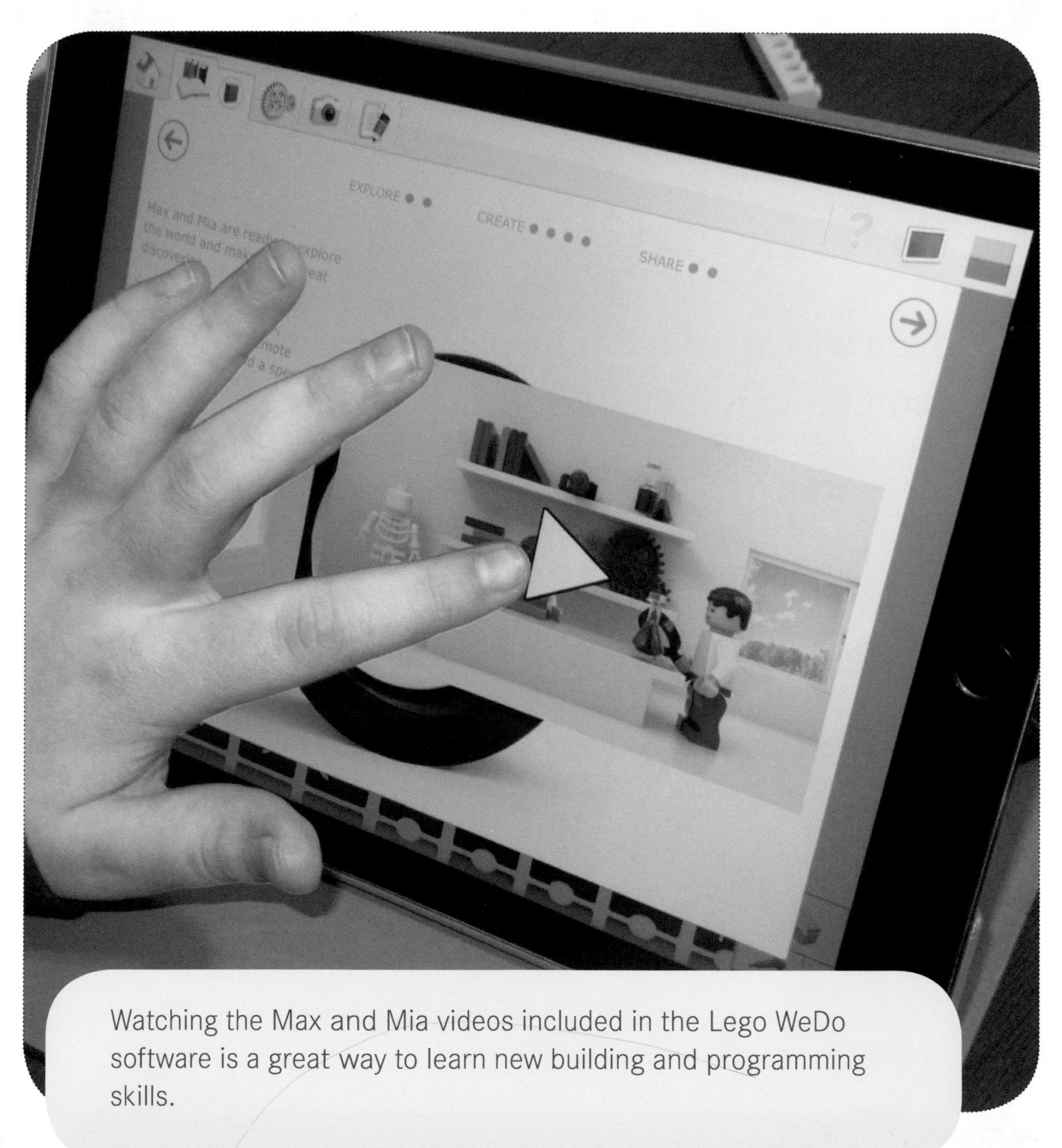

Watching the Max and Mia videos included in the Lego WeDo software is a great way to learn new building and programming skills.

What Is Lego WeDo?

Lego WeDo 2.0 is a kit that has everything you need to build and program different projects. Some projects have step-by-step directions. Others let you use your imagination. You can build things like a robot, a frog, a bee, a helicopter, and a truck. Once you learn the basics, you can also make your own creations!

Max and Mia

The Lego WeDo software comes with helpful videos you can watch. In these videos, Max and Mia are Lego characters that show you how to do things. They love adventures. When you see one of their videos, simply click on the arrow to learn more.

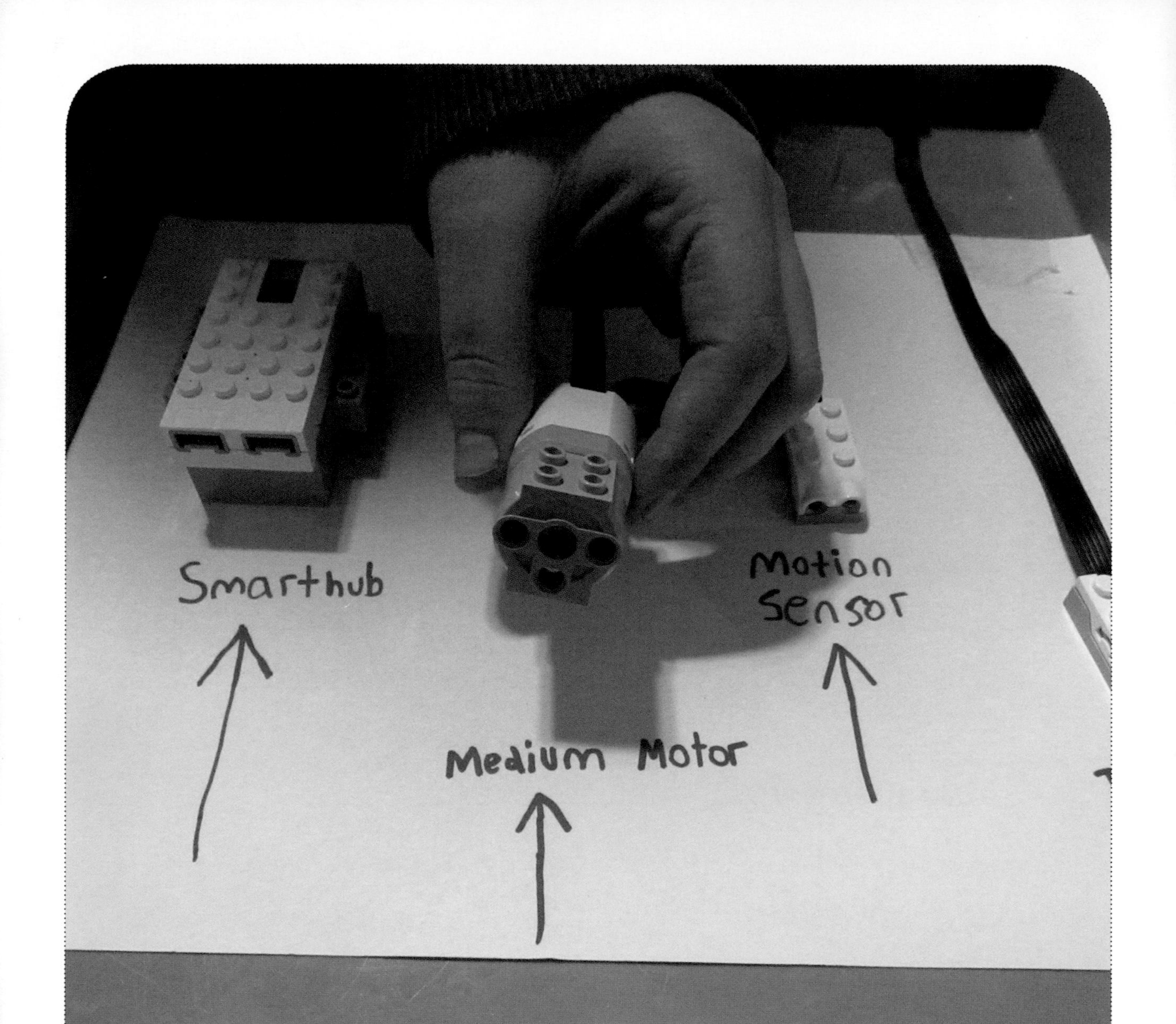

Studs are the bumps on top of a Lego brick. You can use the studs on the Smart Hub, motors, and sensors to connect them to any other Lego pieces.

What's Inside?

Let's look at the most important pieces inside the kit. The Smart Hub is a special programmable Lego brick that connects to motors or **sensors**. It has a light, a place for batteries, and two **ports** for connecting motors and sensors. The medium motor can make things move. It can go slow or fast. It can also turn in different directions. The tilt sensor can tell if your device is moving. The motion sensor can tell when an object is close or far away.

The Milo robot is a great project to start with if you are new to Lego WeDo.

About the Software

Download the Lego WeDo 2.0 software from the Internet. Now, start building your model. Most projects have three steps: Explore, Create, and Share. In the Explore step, you ask questions and get ideas from your life. In the Create step, you find instructions to build and program your model. In the Share step, you share pictures and information with others.

Meet Milo

How would you explore dangerous places such as outer space or the inside of a volcano? In the explore step, you might think about how scientists and **engineers** do this. They actually send robots! In the kit, you will find building instructions to make a **rover** just like a scientist would! Its name is Milo.

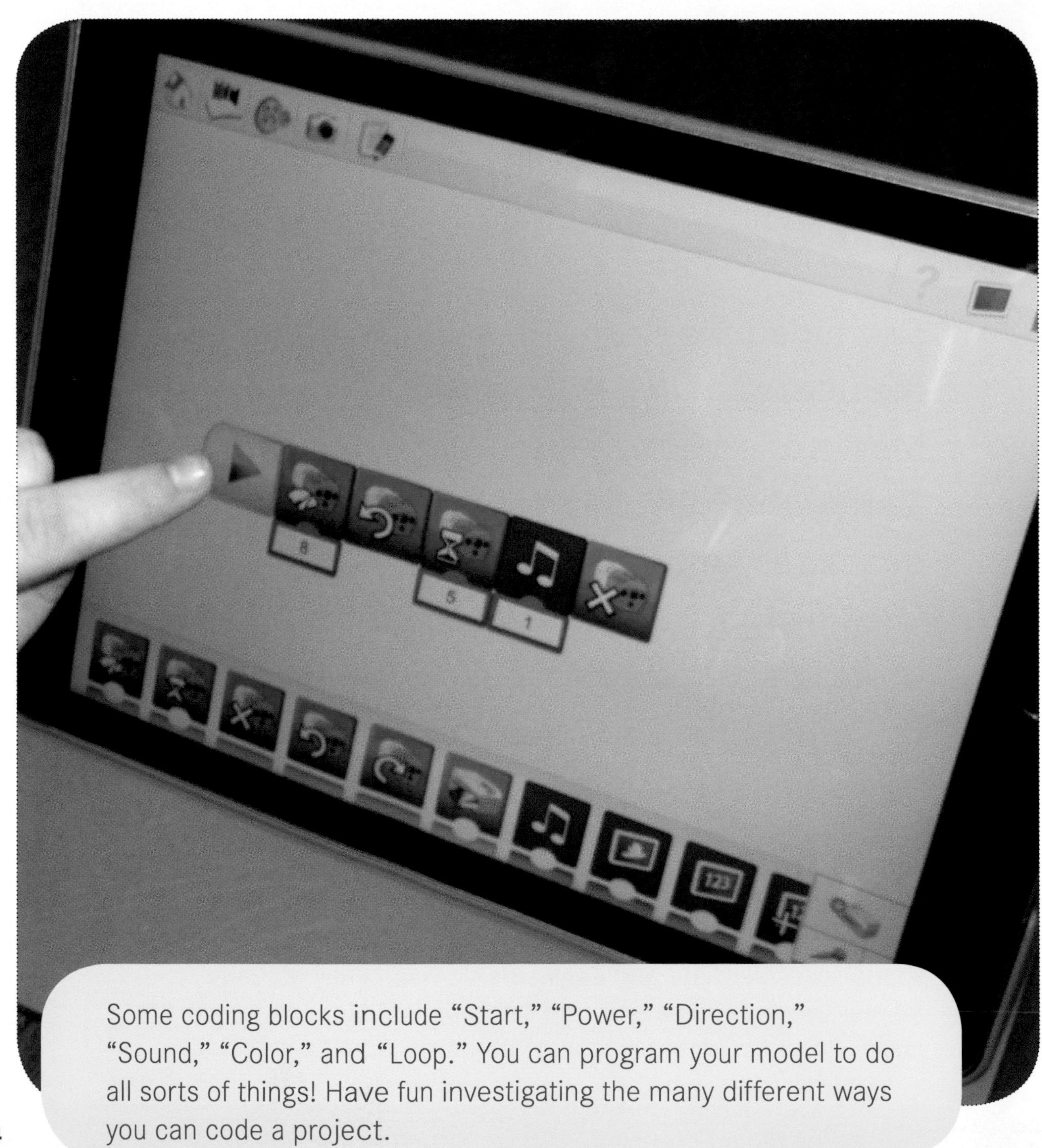

Some coding blocks include “Start,” “Power,” “Direction,” “Sound,” “Color,” and “Loop.” You can program your model to do all sorts of things! Have fun investigating the many different ways you can code a project.

Time to Program

Once your Lego model is built, you are ready to program it. A program is the **code** you use to make your model do something. The coding blocks at the bottom of the screen have pictures to help you understand what they do. Simply drag and drop the code blocks where you want them to go. In the Create step, there are sample programs that you can try. It is also fun to create your own!

Working together will help you solve problems faster and come up with new ideas.

Teamwork Is Key

Working with a friend makes building and programming fun. You can share ideas and talk about different ways to build or program your model. When building, one person can find the bricks you need while the other person puts them together. Then you can switch jobs. In the Share step, you will find ideas for sharing your discoveries with other Lego WeDo users.

Try turning Milo into a rabbit to extend your project!

Extending Your Project

Once you know the basics of building and programming, you can use those ideas for new projects. In the design library, you will find ways to extend your ideas. The design library will inspire you to try things such as making your robot spin, wobble, crank, lift, and push. Use these ideas to create something amazing!

Making Old Projects New Again

Try making changes to an existing project. For example, think about how you can change Milo into an animal that moves. The programming would be similar. All you would need to do is change how you build it.

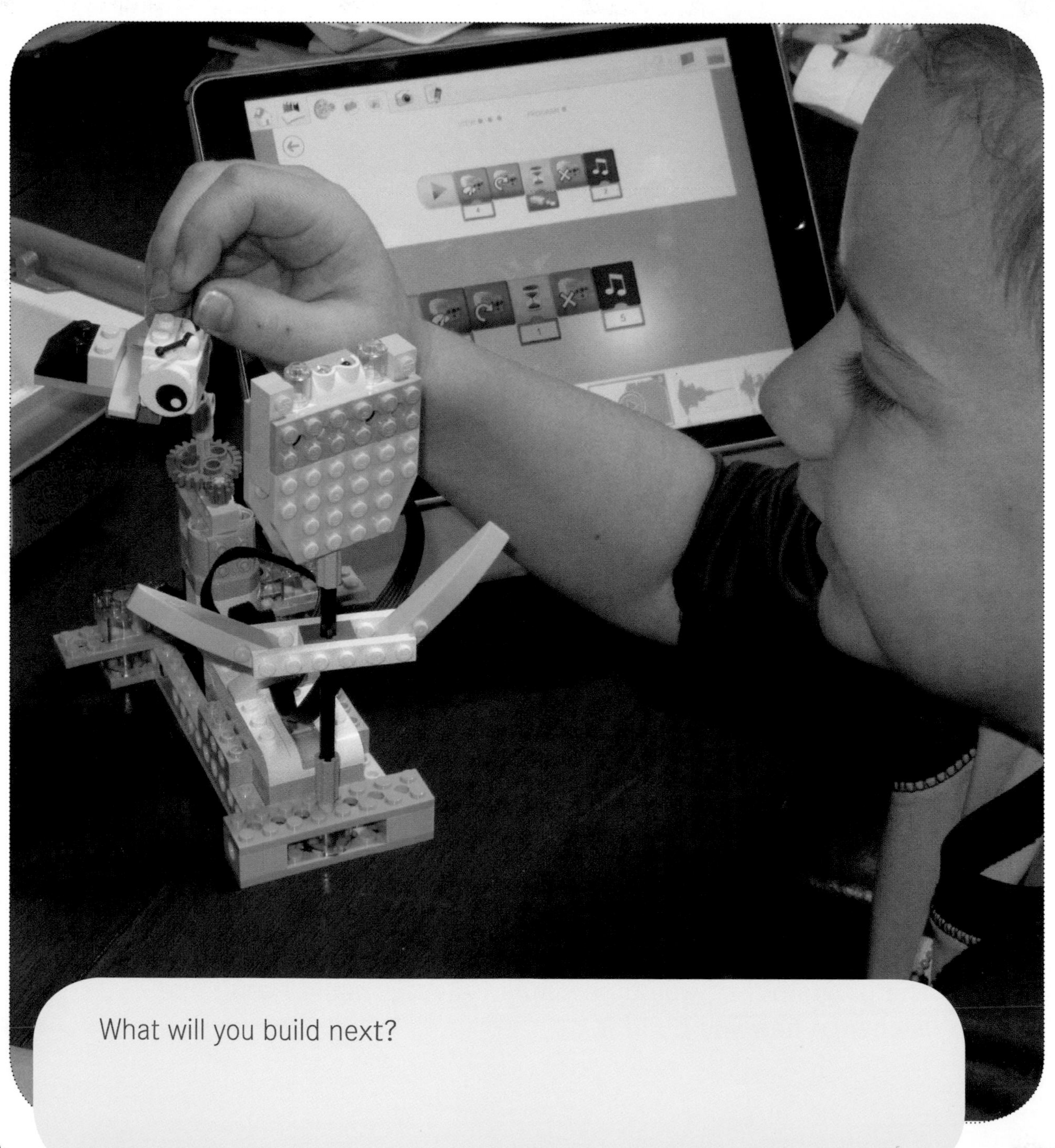

What will you build next?

Conclusion

Building and programming with Lego WeDo 2.0 is easy and fun. You will amaze your friends and family. Share what you have made, and inspire them to make their own motorized Lego creations!

Glossary

code (KODE) instructions for a computer, written in a programming language

engineers (en-juh-NEERZ) people who use knowledge of science, math, and technology to design and build solutions to practical problems

motorized (MOH-tur-izd) powered by a motor

ports (PORTS) places on a computer or other device that are designed to fit different kinds of plugs and cables

rover (ROH-vur) a robot used to explore places that are difficult or dangerous for humans to reach, such as other planets

sensors (SEN-surz) instruments that can detect and measure changes in distance, light, sound, or other things and send the information to a computer or other device

software (SAWFT-wair) a computer program

Books

Lovett, Amber. *Coding with Blockly*. Ann Arbor, MI: Cherry Lake Publishing, 2017.

Matteson, Adrienne. *Coding with ScratchJr*. Ann Arbor, MI: Cherry Lake Publishing, 2017.

Web Sites

Hour of Code
https://hourofcode.com/us
Learn more about coding by completing a variety of activities.

ScratchJr
www.scratchjr.org
Create interactive stories and games with the ScratchJr programming language.

Index

About the Author

Amy Quinn is a first-grade teacher in West Bloomfield, Michigan. She is also a coach and mentor for FIRST LEGO League and a team manager for Destination Imagination. Amy has a daughter named Emily and a son named Tommy who both love to design and create new things!